Now I Know

Tick Tock Clock

Written by Sharon Gordon

Illustrated by Don Page

Troll Associates

Library of Congress Cataloging in Publication Data

Gordon, Sharon.
    Tick tock clock.

    (Now I know)
    Summary: A lonely grandfather clock finds a friend.
    [1. Clocks and watches—Fiction] I. Page, Don, ill.
II. Title.
PZ7.G65936Ti   [E]   81-11393
ISBN 0-89375-676-8   AACR2
ISBN 0-89375-677-6 (pbk.)

10   9   8   7   6   5

Tick-tock goes the clock.

What time is it?

The grandfather clock goes tick- tock.

Tick-tock goes the minute.

Tick-tock goes the hour.

Minute after minute . . . hour after hour . . .

tick after tock . . . the grandfather clock tells time.

But the grandfather clock is lonely.
The grandfather clock has no one.
Tick-tock goes the clock.

Tick-tock . . . the clock stopped!

The grandfather clock stopped ticking.
What time is it?

No one knows the minute.

No one knows the hour.
No one knows the time!

"Tell the clock doctor!"

"Tell the clock doctor the clock has stopped."

"Hmm . . . his tick is fine."

"His tock is fine."

"What is wrong with the grandfather clock?"

"Hmm . . . look here, look here."

"Look what is here."

"Here is why the clock stopped."

Now the grandfather clock has someone.

He is not lonely now.

Tick-tock goes the minute.

Tick-tock goes the hour.

The grandfather clock is fine.

The grandfather clock tells time.

What time is it?

What time is it?